WHO WILL EMMET ASK TO HELP HIM? USE THE CLUES BELOW TO FIND OUT!

IT DEFINITELY WON'T BE A DUPLO CREATURE!

THIS PERSON IS NOT A PIRATE ...

... DOESN'T HAVE ANY HORNS ...

... WEARS A MASK ...

... AND ISN'T WEARING BLUE!

LUCY  **UNIKITTY** **DUPLO CREATURE**

BENNY **BATMAN** **METALBEARD**

WHICH ROUTE SHOULD THE FRIENDS TAKE TO REACH BATMAN'S BASE? ADD UP THE POINTS ON EACH PATH AND YOU'LL FIND OUT THE ANSWER. THE ROAD WITH THE LEAST POINTS WINS.

8   7   9

3

HOW MANY?

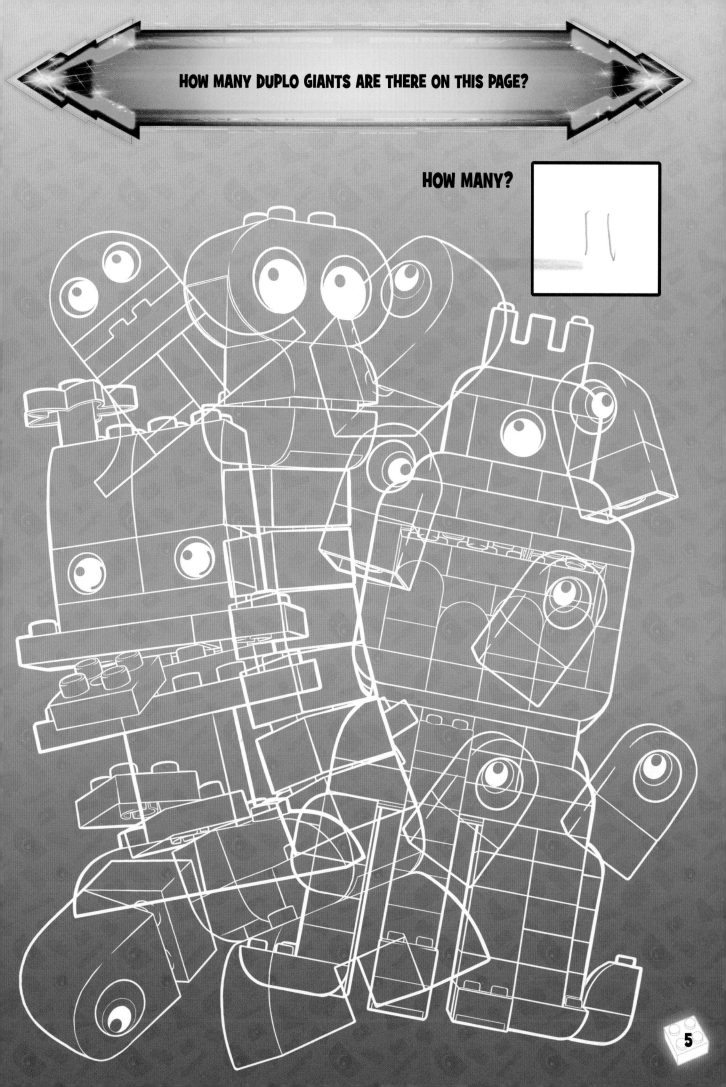

BATMAN IS READY TO ATTACK! HE JUST NEEDS TO FIND SOME THINGS IN THIS MESS: SEVEN BATARANGS, TWO GRAPPLE GUNS AND THE KEY TO THE BATMOBILE.

WE'VE GOT BRICKS TOO, DUDE!

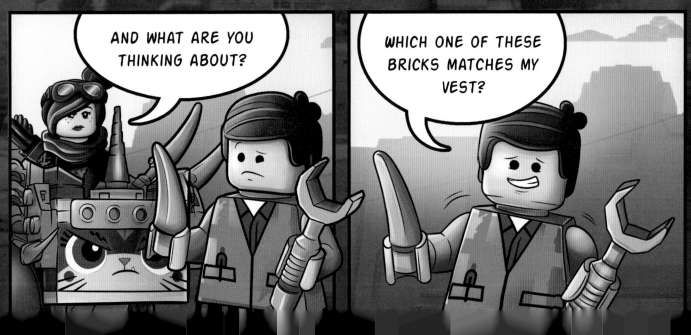

CAN YOU SPOT SEVEN DIFFERENCES BETWEEN THESE TWO PICTURES?

I GET LOTS OF ANGRY THOUGHTS WHEN I LOOK AT THE GENERAL ON THE NEXT PAGE!

WHICH OF THE HELMETS IS IDENTICAL TO THE ONE THAT SWEET MAYHEM IS WEARING?

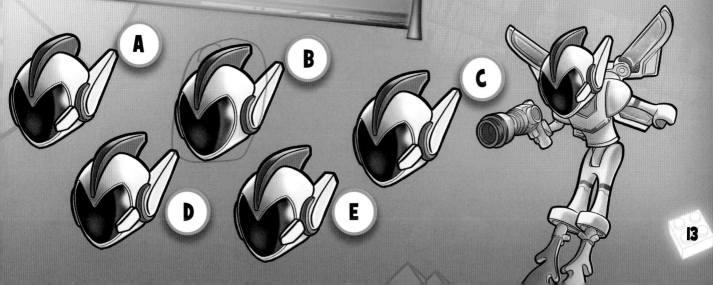

A

B

C

D

E

DESIGN A MACHINE OR VEHICLE YOU THINK WOULD HELP DEFEAT THE MYSTERIOUS SPACESHIP!

Name... Jeff

TO BUILD IT YOU WILL NEED PARTS OF YOUR OWN DESIGN AS WELL AS: A BANANA, TWO CANNONS AND FOUR PIZZAS.

14

SWEET MAYHEM IS CONTINUING THE ATTACK. DRAW TWO STRAIGHT LINES TO DIVIDE THE WHITE RECTANGLE INTO THREE PARTS, WITH TWO STARS AND TWO HEARTS IN EACH PART.

COMPLETE THESE SEQUENCES BY WRITING THE CORRECT LETTERS FROM THE GENERAL'S POSES AT THE BOTTOM OF THE PAGE INTO THE BLANK SPACES.

SWEET MAYHEM HAS CAUGHT THE HEROES! UNTANGLE THE LINES TO SEE WHO AVOIDED BEING TAKEN.

EMMET IS SETTING OFF ON A JOURNEY TO SAVE HIS FRIENDS. FOLLOW THE ARROWS INDICATING THE DIRECTION AND THE NUMBER OF SQUARES YOU NEED TO COVER. YOU'LL SOON REACH SWEET MAYHEM'S VEHICLE.

MATCH THE MISSING PUZZLE PIECES TO THE PICTURE OF EMMET FLYING IN HIS SPACESHIP.

A B C D

LOOK AT THESE SHAPES AND CHOOSE THE ONE THAT MATCHES EMMET'S VEHICLE.

B C D

A E

HURRY UP! WE'VE GOT A MISSION TO COMPLETE!

FINISH

VEST FRIENDS OR NO, YOU'RE MY HERO!!!

HAVE YOU EVER TRIED DRAWING A RAPTOR TRAINER? HERE'S YOUR CHANCE! FOLLOW THE INSTRUCTIONS BELOW.

SKETCH SIMPLE SHAPES FOR THE OUTLINE OF THE HEAD, NECK AND SHOULDERS.

1.

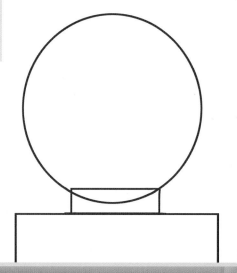

DRAW THE CHARACTER'S SHAPE WITH A THICKER LINE.

2.

ADD THE EYES AND THE MOUTH.

3.

DON'T FORGET THE STUBBLE!

4.

HEY! PRACTISE HERE!

TO CONVINCE THE HEROES TO STAY WITH HER, QUEEN WATEVRA WA'NABI PROMISED EACH OF THEM THE THING THEY DREAMED OF. CONNECT THE DOTS TO SEE WHAT THINGS SHE PROMISED BENNY AND METALBEARD.

YOU ARE THE SPECIAL AND YOU DECIDE!

PLEASE REX! HELP ME REACH THE SYSTAR DIMENSION AND RESCUE MY FRIENDS.

I'M NOT GOING BACK THERE! IT MADE ME FEEL SO LONELY!

COME ON, IF YOU TEACH ME HOW TO BE TOUGH, WE CAN BE A TEAM.

OK, THAT SOUNDS GOOD! FASTEN YOUR VEST. THROUGH THE STAIRGATE TO THE SYSTAR DIMENSION WE GO!

I SUSPECT YOUR FRIENDS WERE TAKEN BY AN ALIEN QUEEN AND THEY'RE ON ONE OF THESE PLANETS. JUST TELL ME WHICH ONE.

ME?

SURE! YOU ARE THE SPECIAL AND YOU DECIDE.

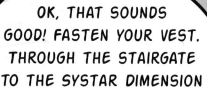

WHAT IF I'M WRONG?

JUST POINT TO ONE OF THE PLANETS AND BE CONFIDENT. THAT'S WHAT THE SPECIAL DOES.

OK! LET'S SAY IT'S ... THIS ONE!

HA! I KNOW THIS PLANET! IT'S FULL OF HOSTILE ALIENS, WHO DREAM OF TORMENTING ...

... AND BRAINWASHING US. IT'S GONNA BE SO MUCH FUN!

I CAN'T WAIT!

UMM ... I JUST REALISED THE SPECIAL DIDN'T CHOOSE THE RIGHT ONE! CAN I HAVE ANOTHER GO?

ANSWERS

2–3

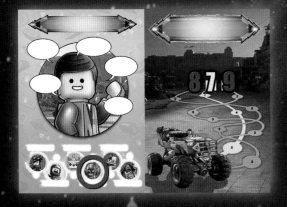

4–5

6–7

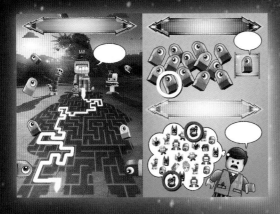

8

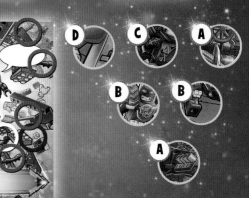

9

D C A

B B

A

12–13

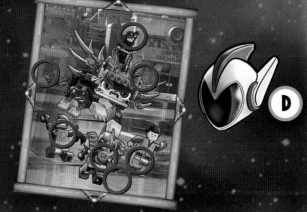

D

15

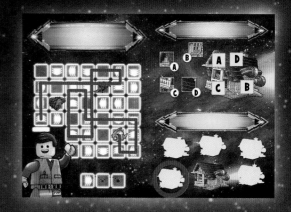